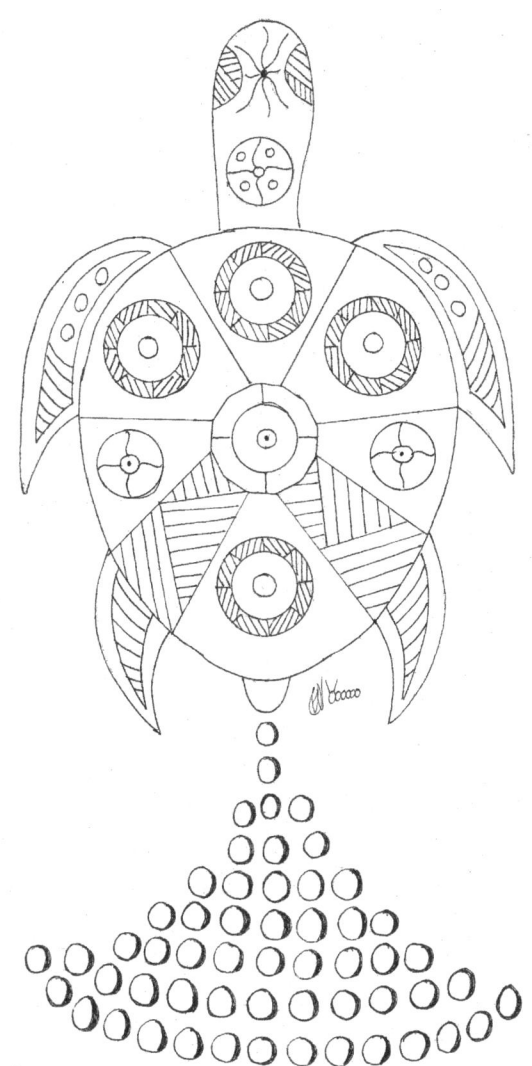

Aboriginal Colouring Designs

by Dawnie

ISBN: 1539970434
ISBN-13: 978-1539970439
Published By Noel Downs Publishing

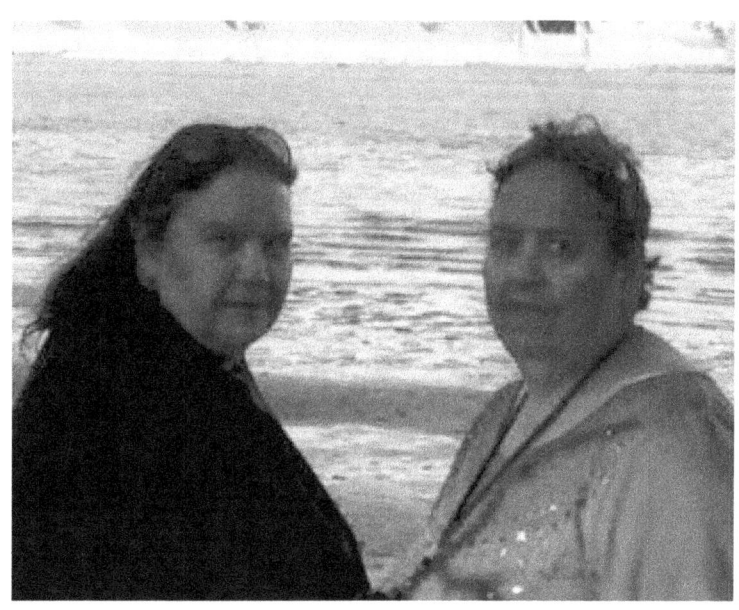

DEDICATION

This book is dedicated to my sister Helen Elizabeth Williams (nee Wortley) who we sadly lost to leukemia on 4th May 2016. She will be sadly missed.   Forever in my heart.   Until we meet again Sis.
Sharon (Dawnie) Wortley

.

ACKNOWLEDGMENTS

For their ongoing support and encouragement
So many thanks to my family with special thanks to my sister Jean.
Thank you.

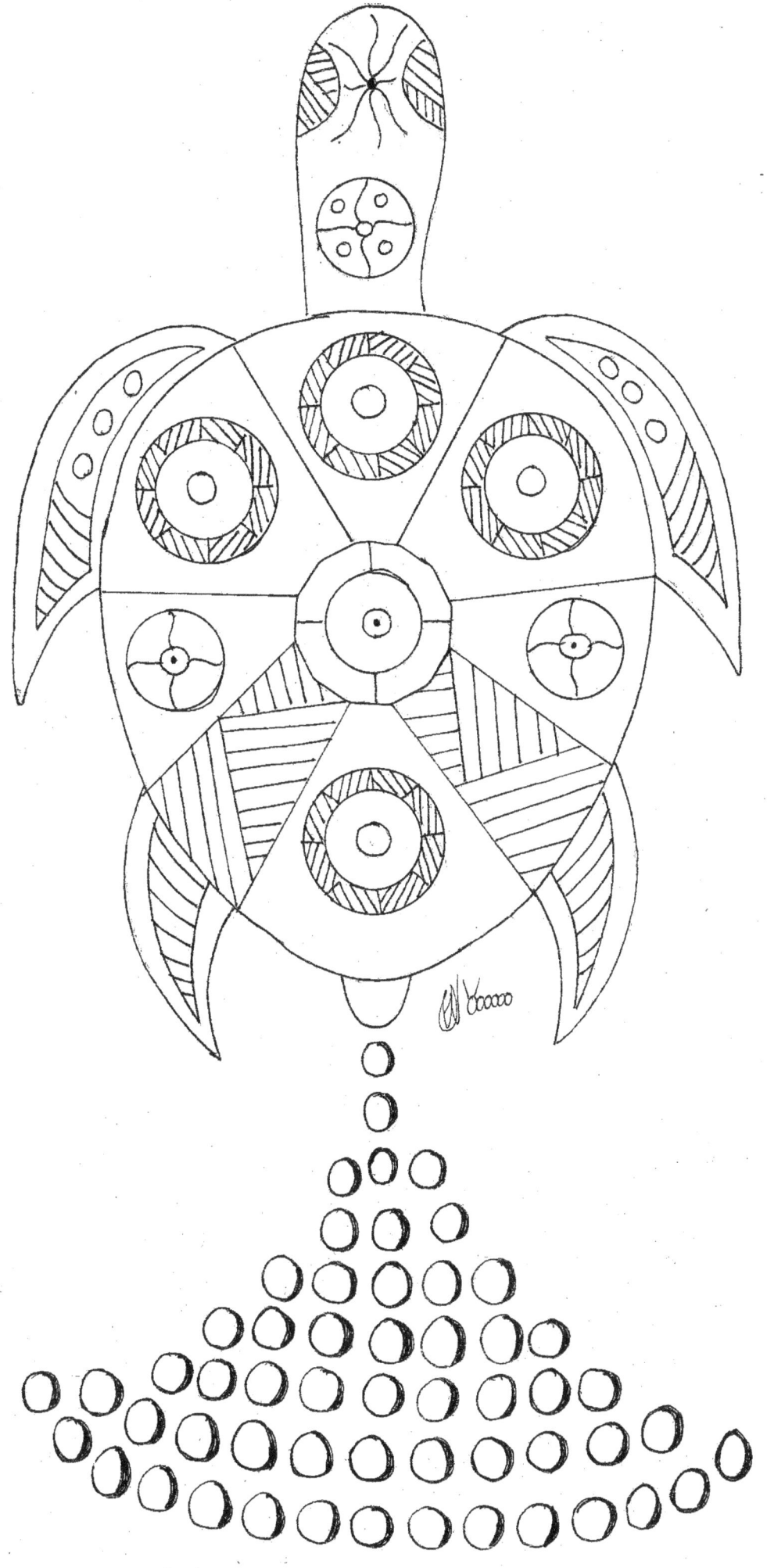

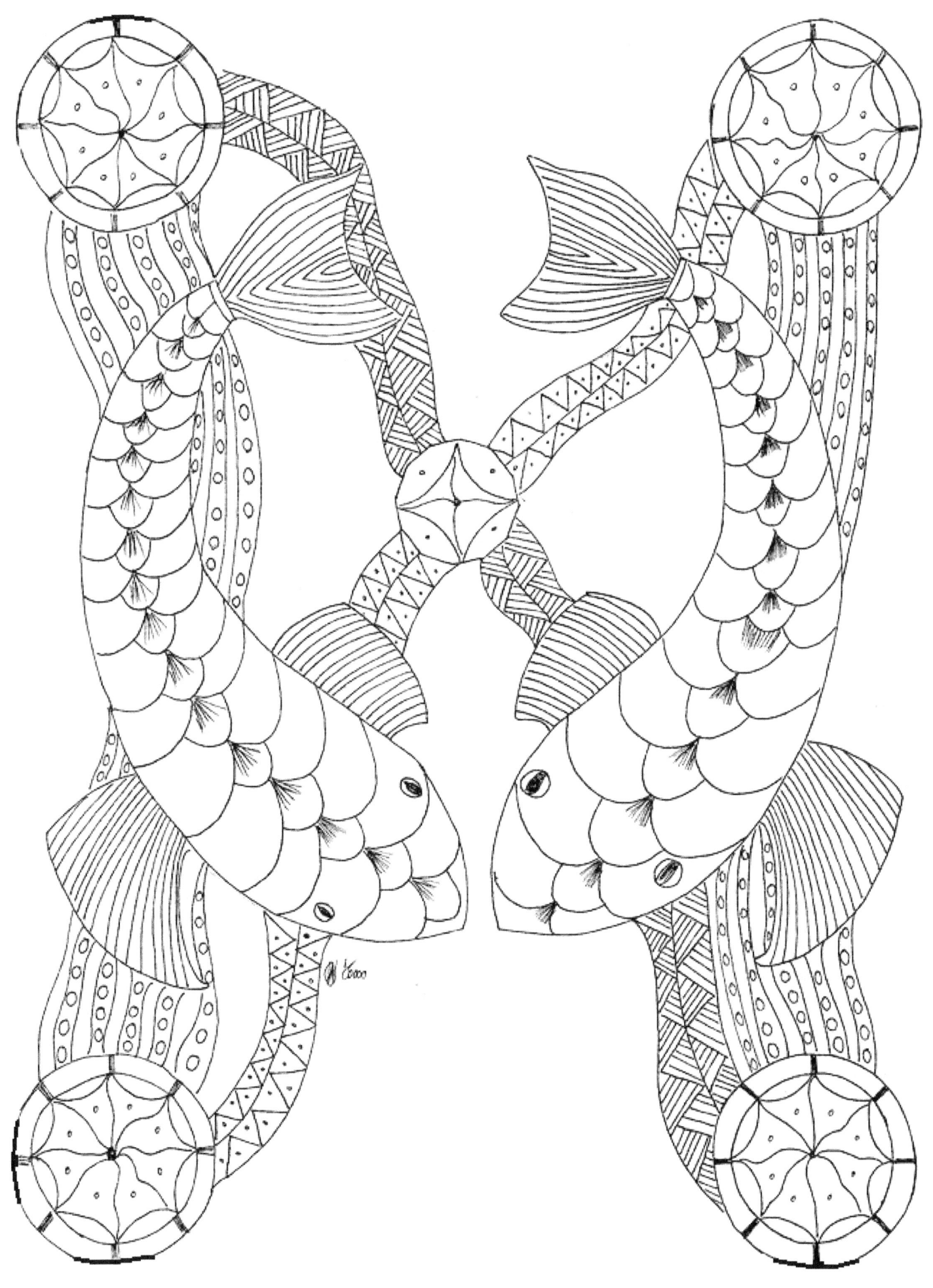

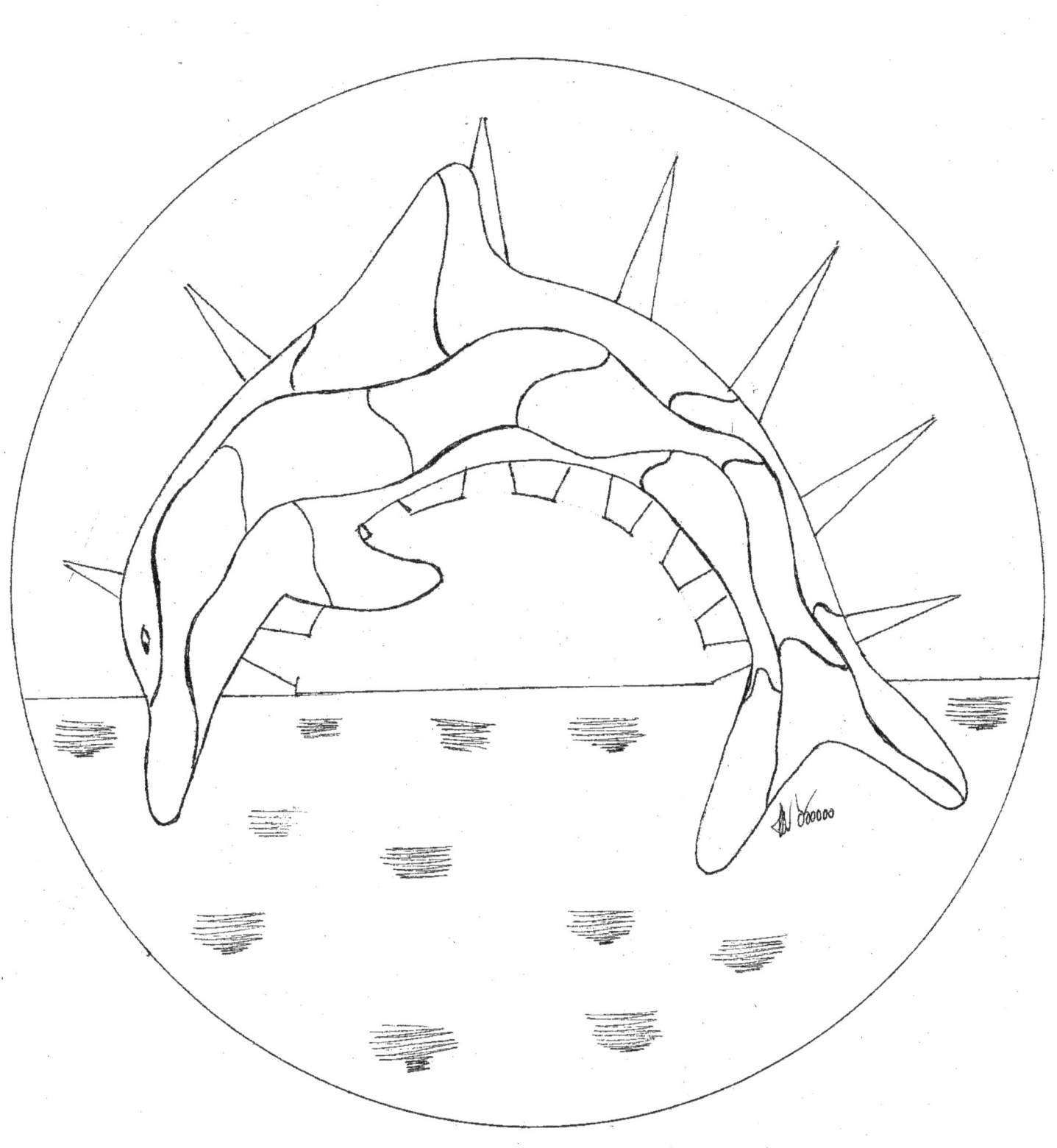

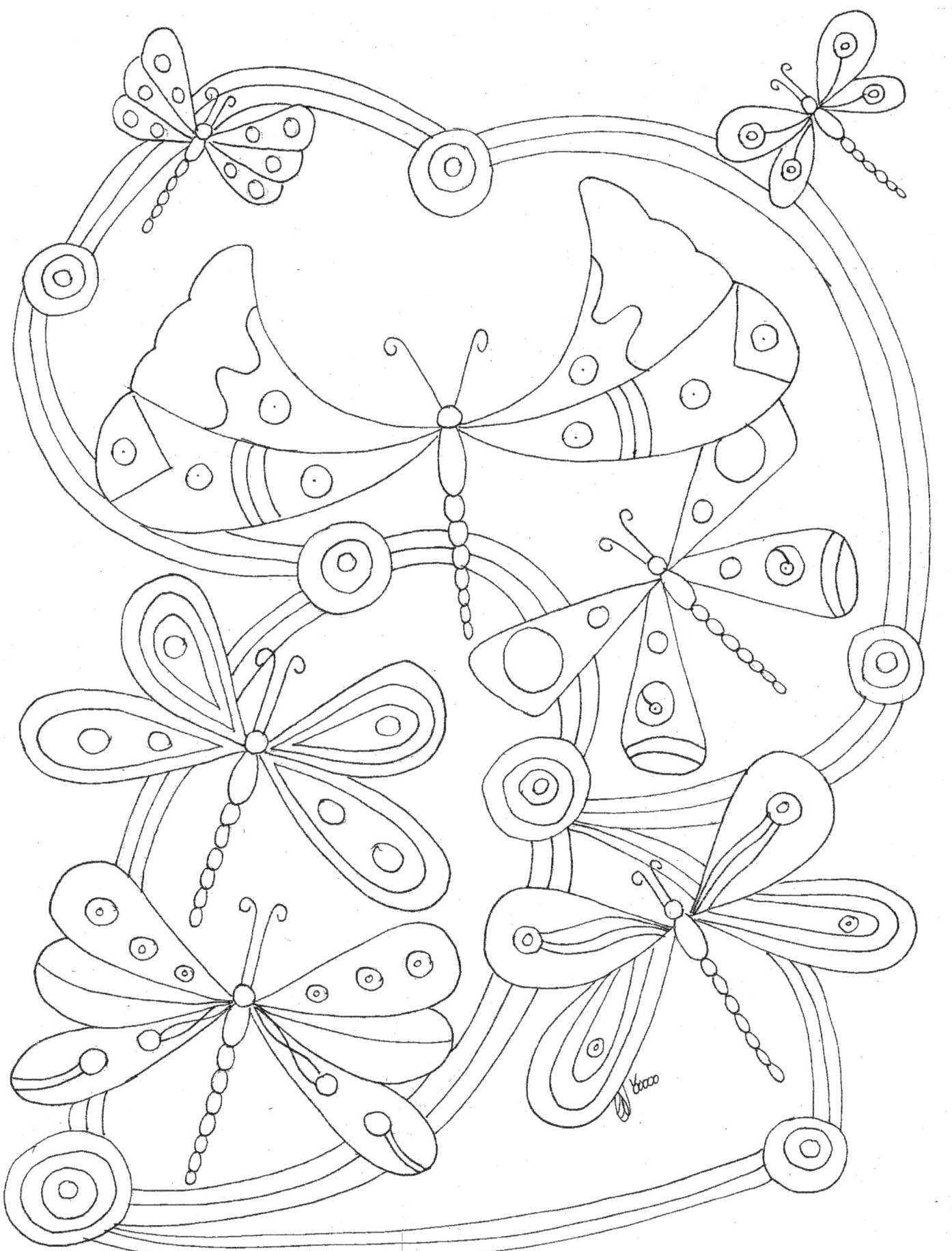

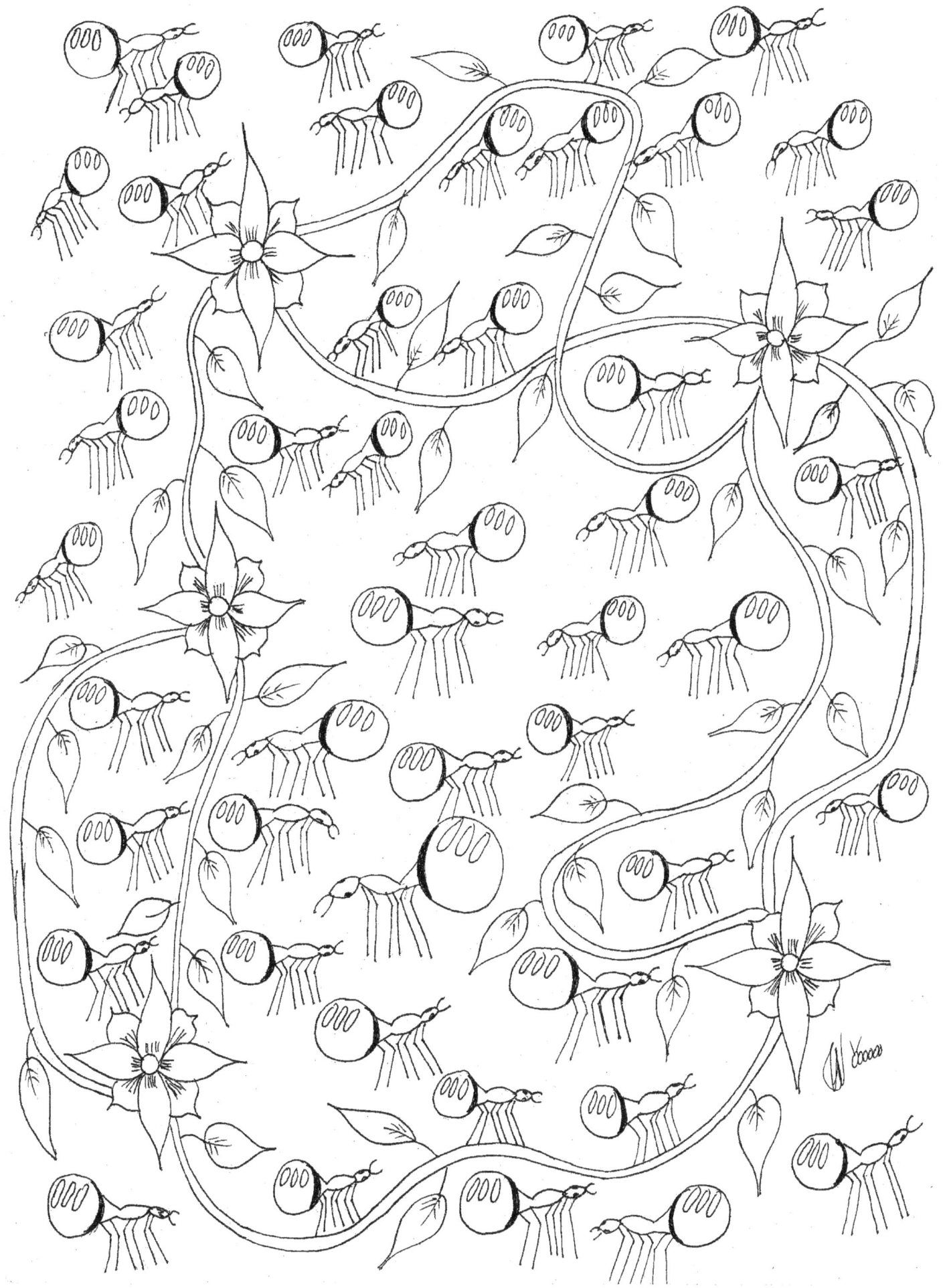

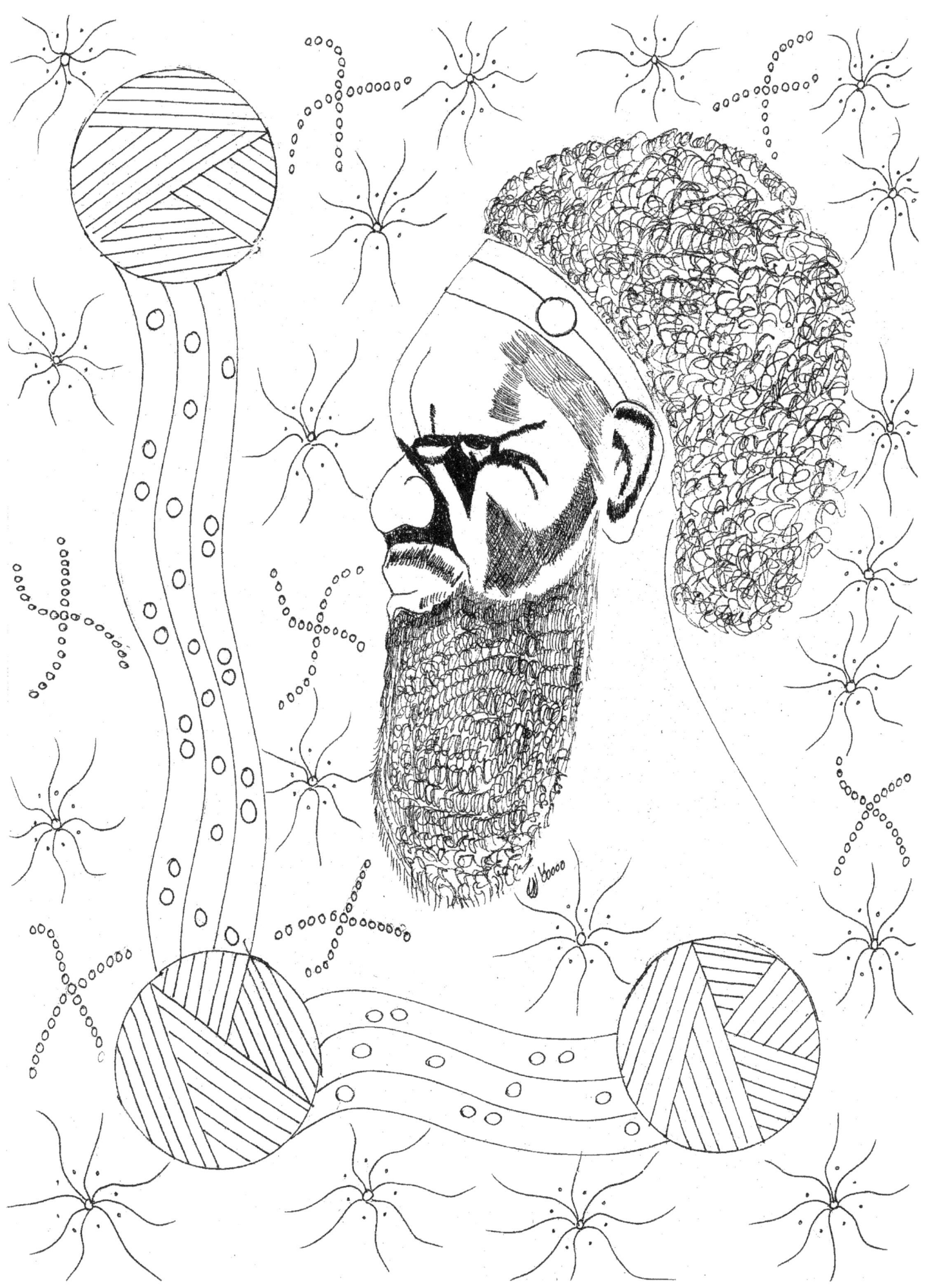

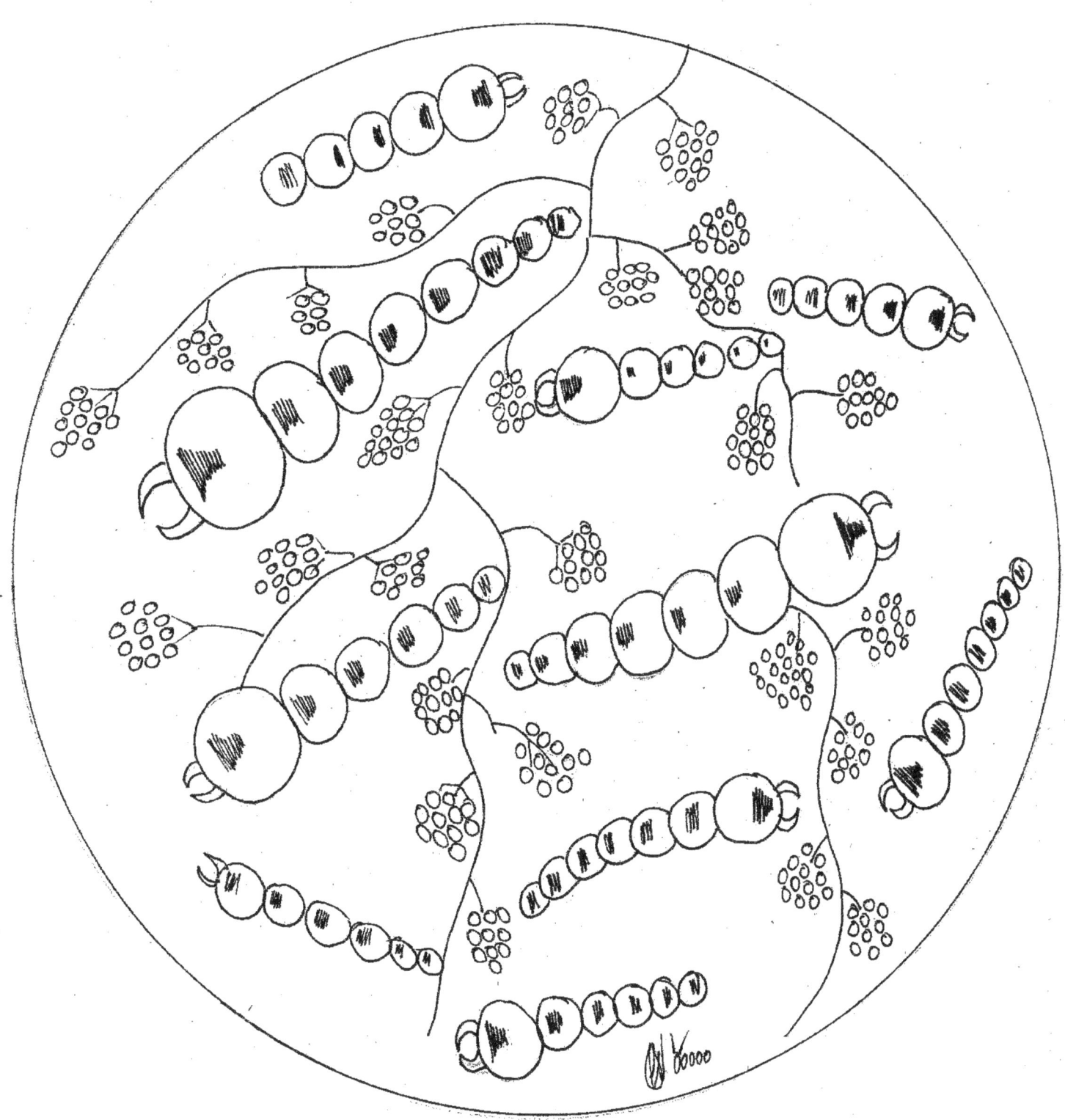

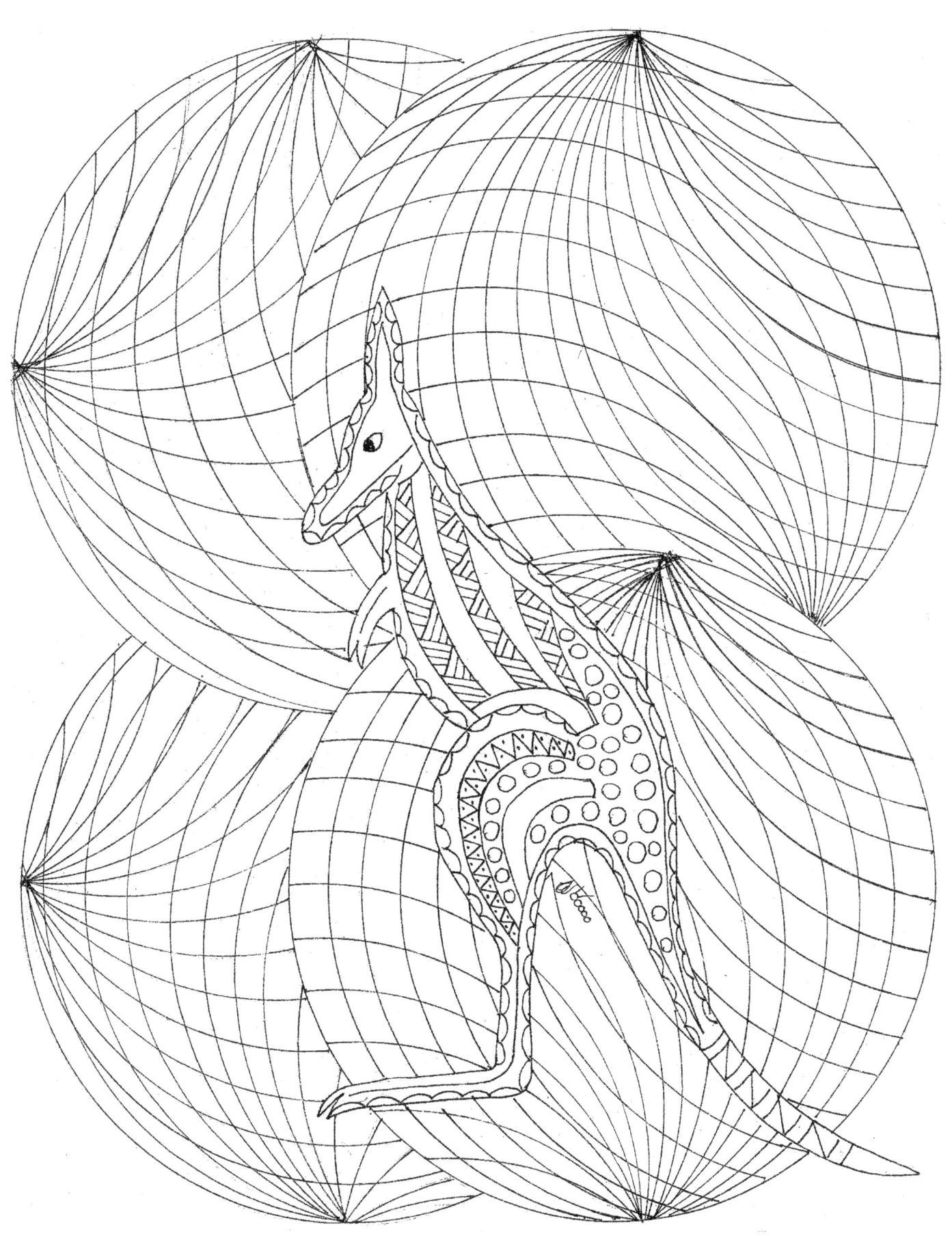

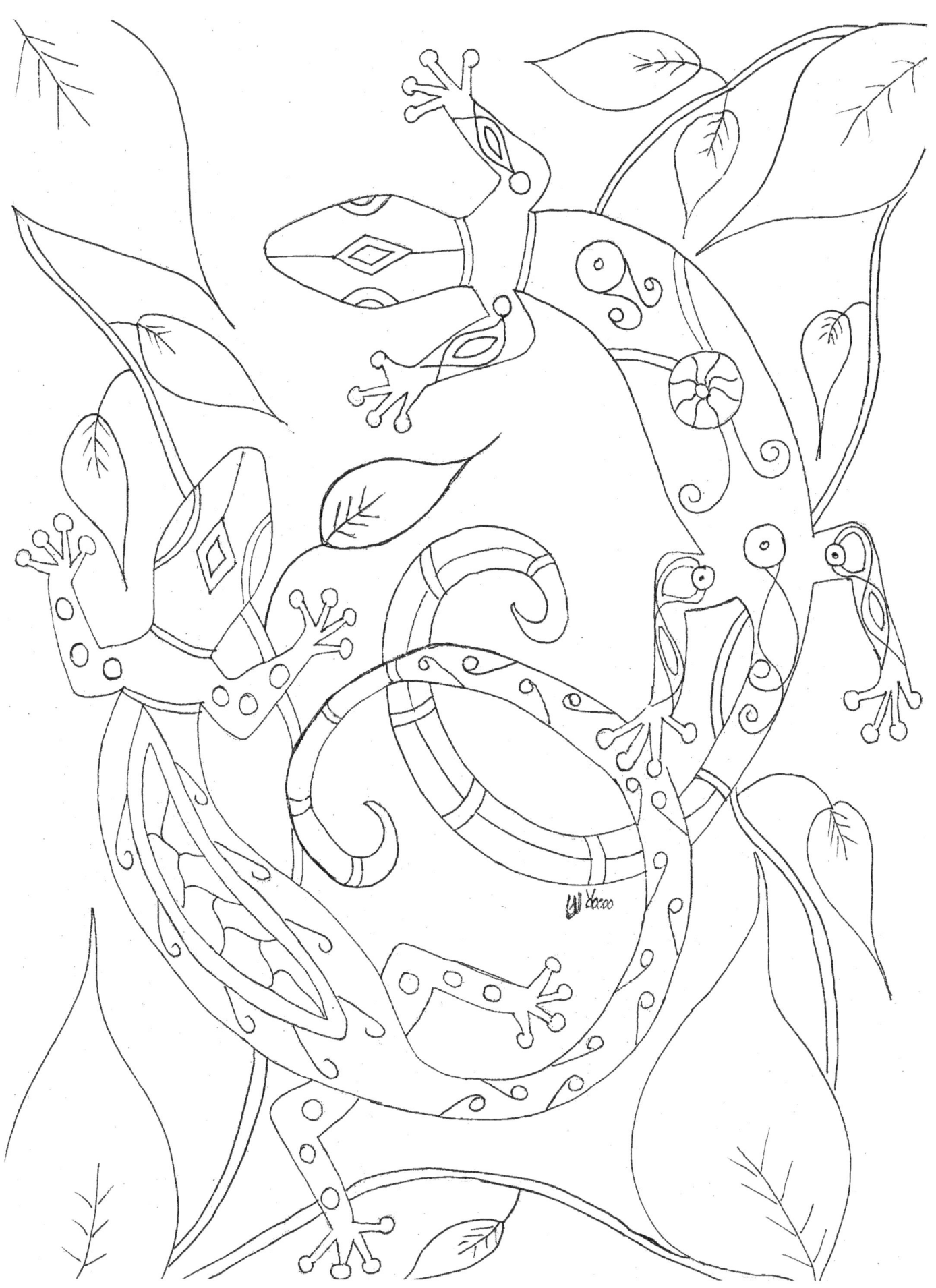

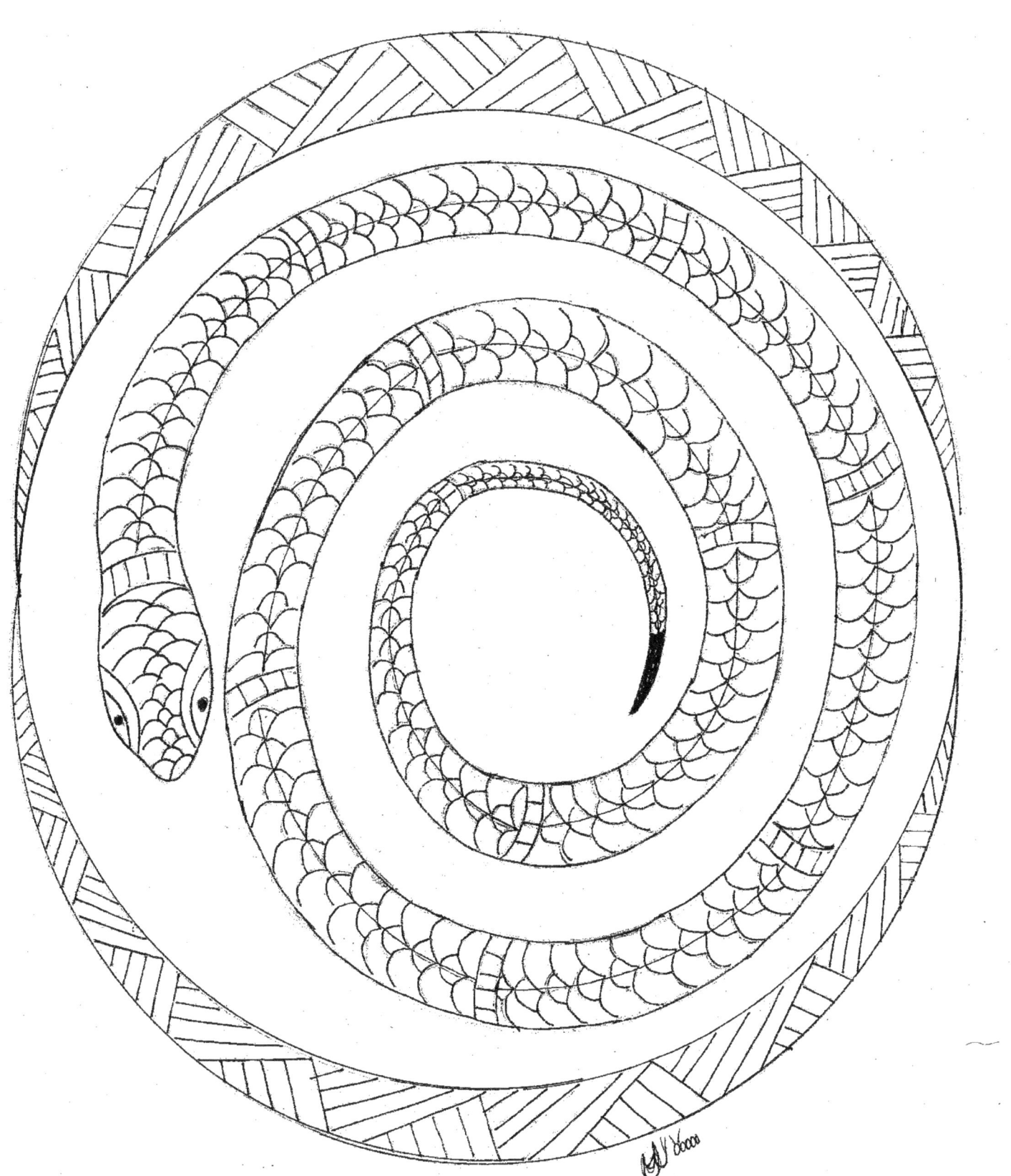

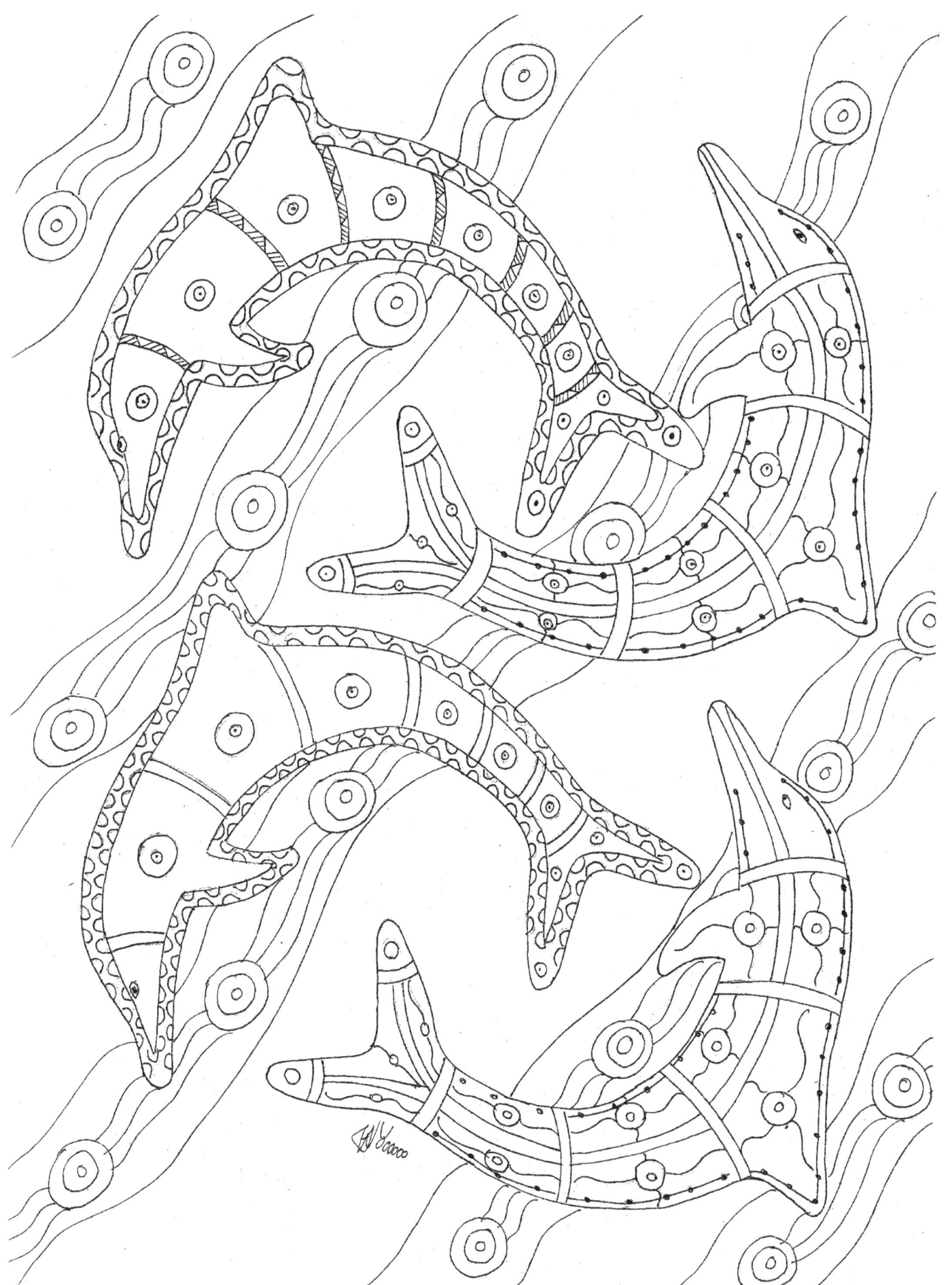

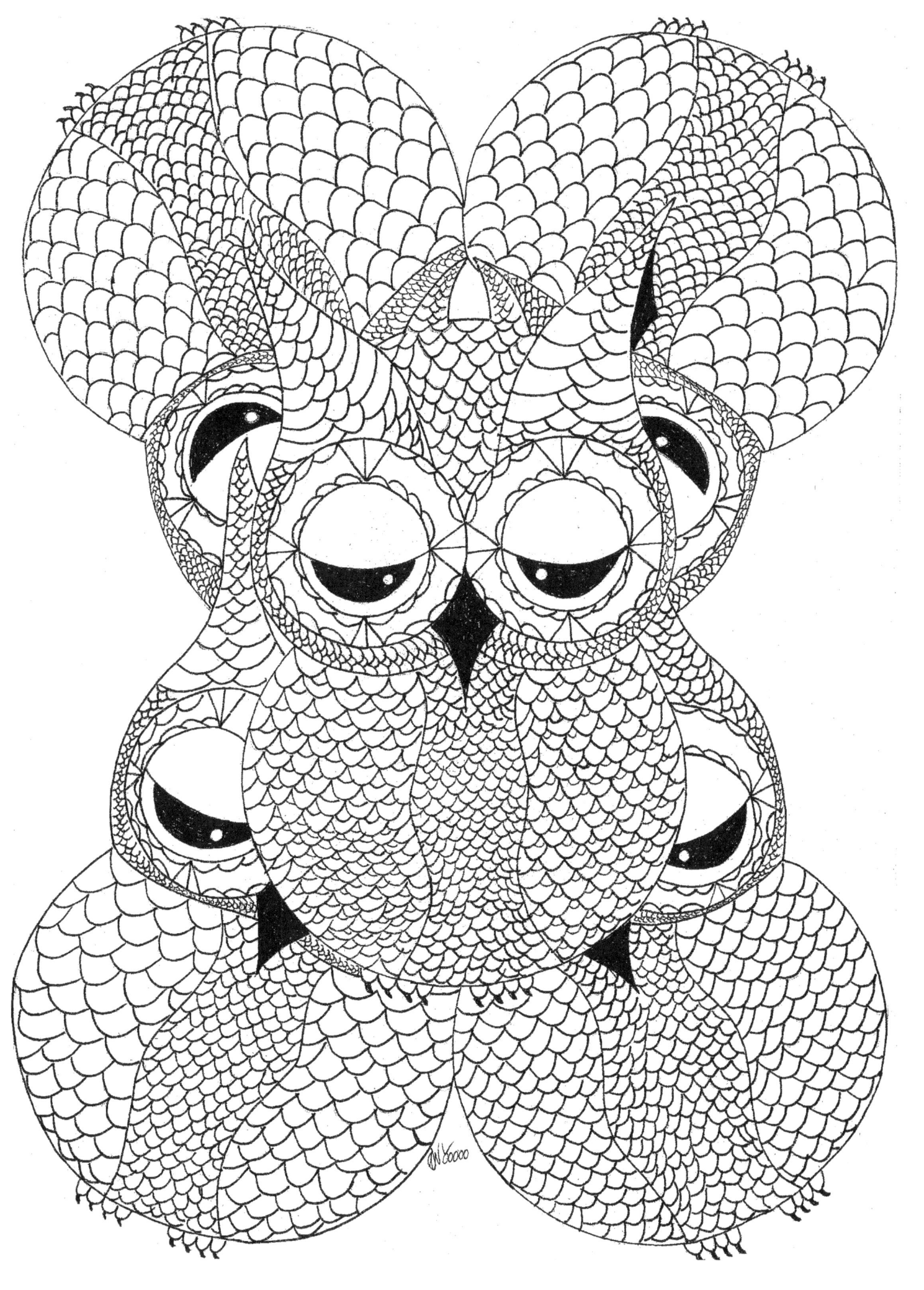

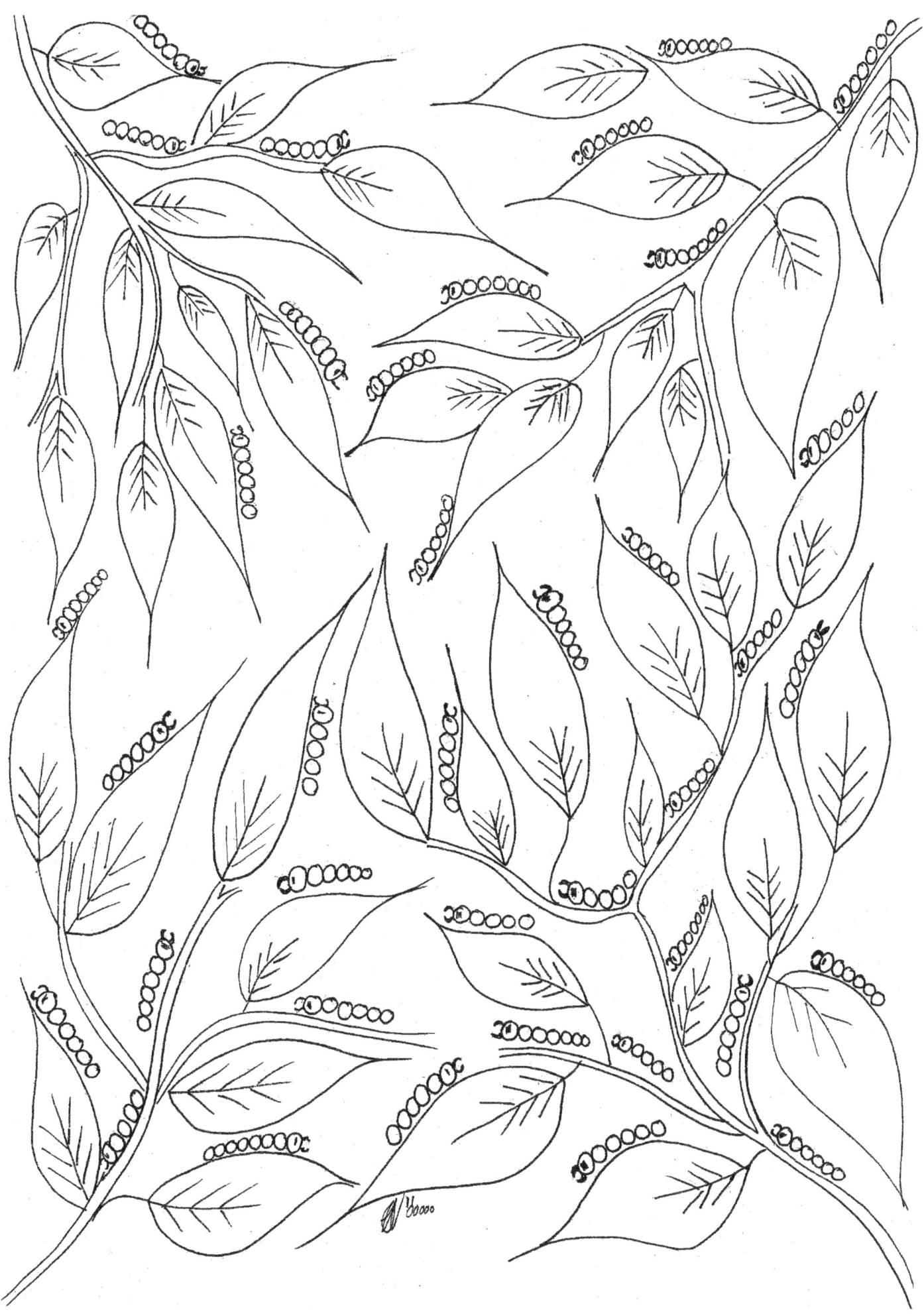

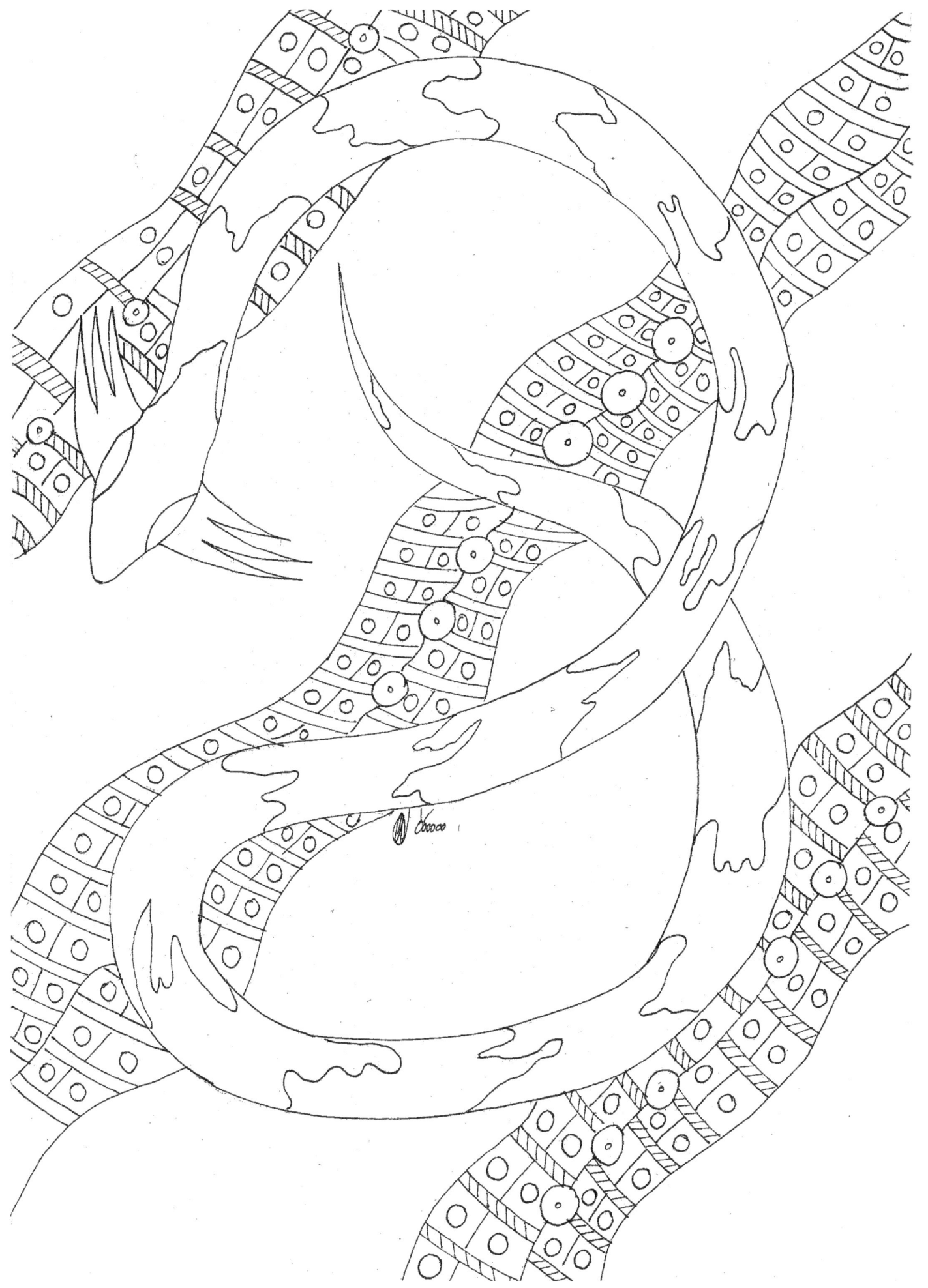

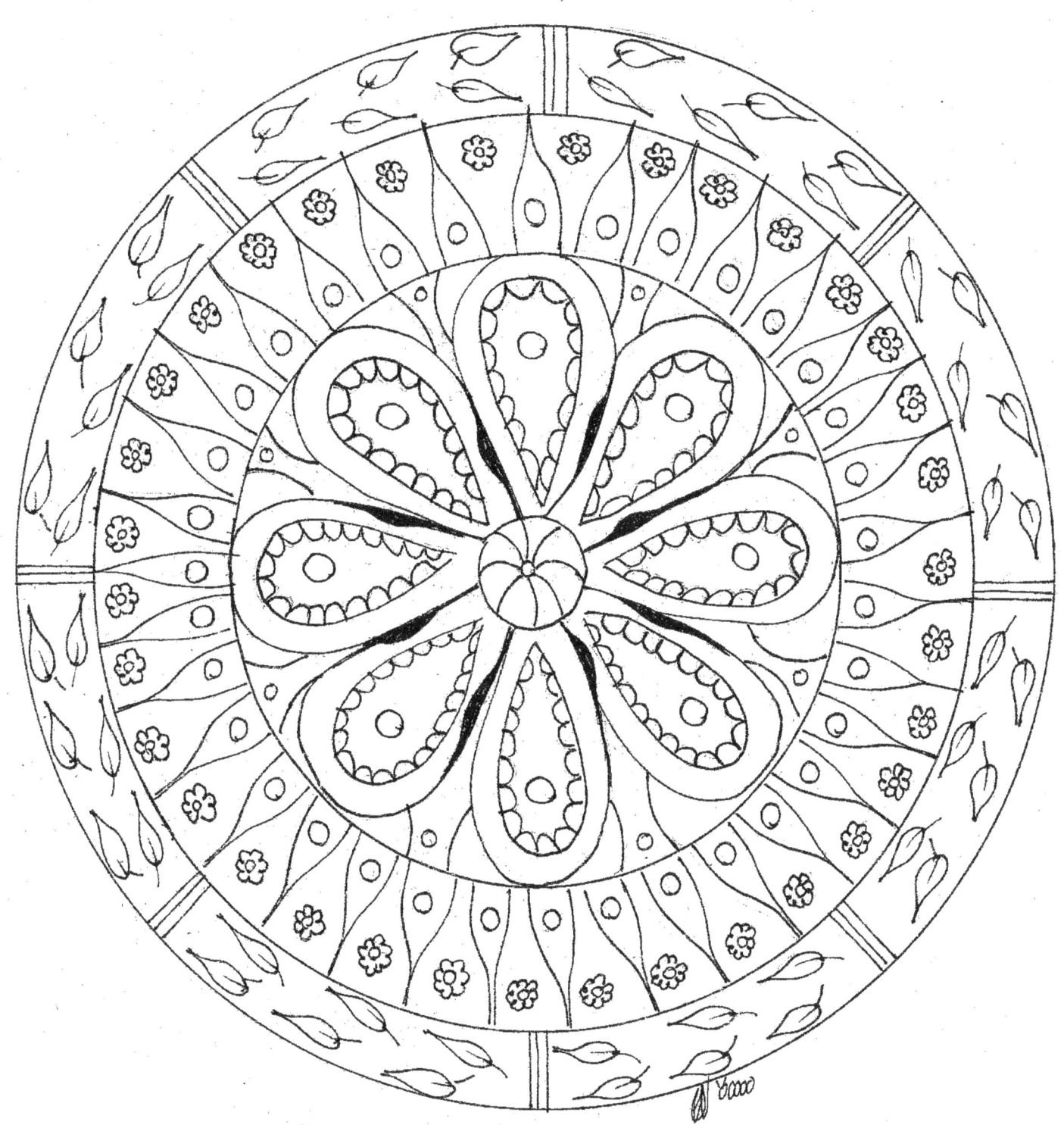

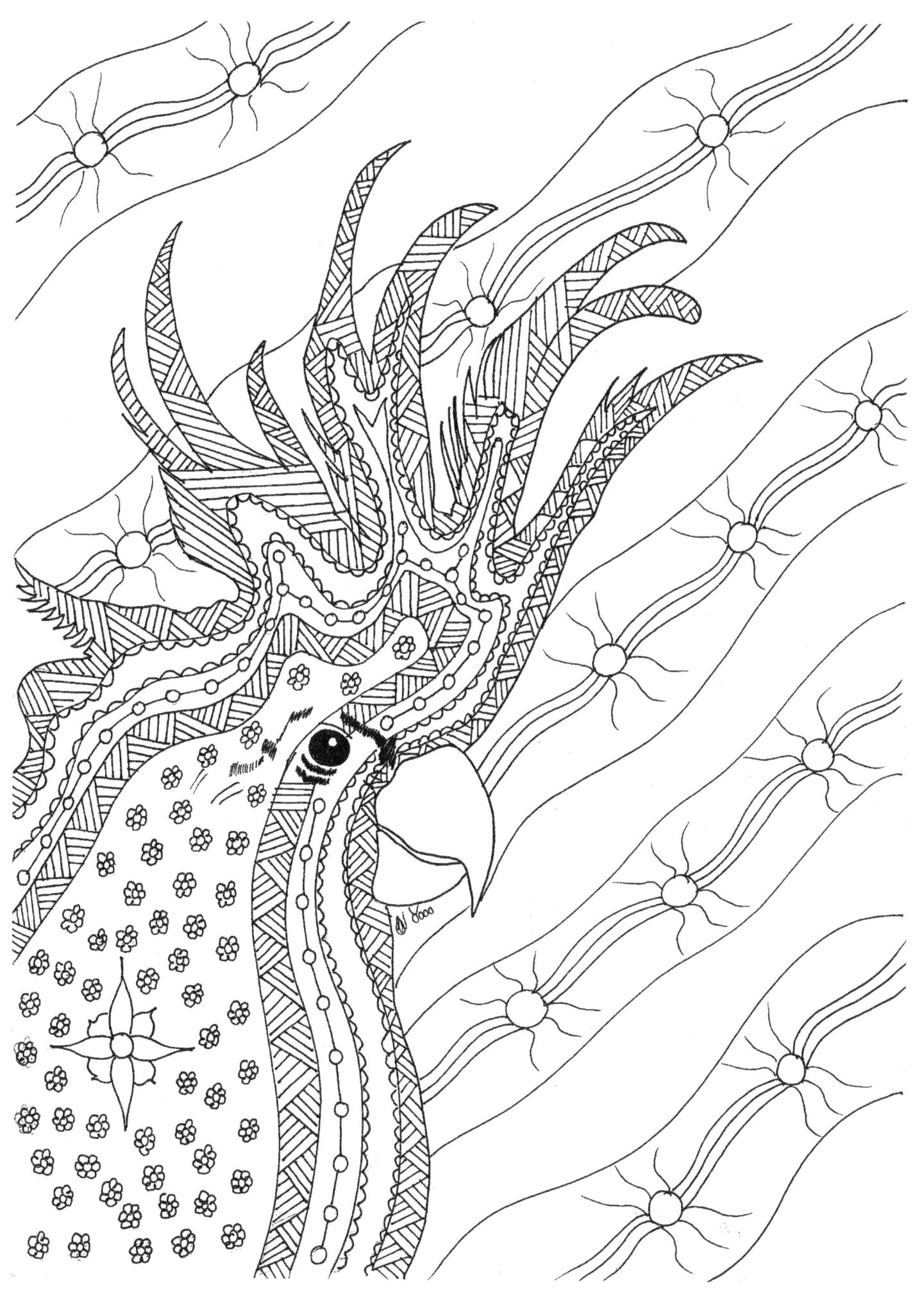

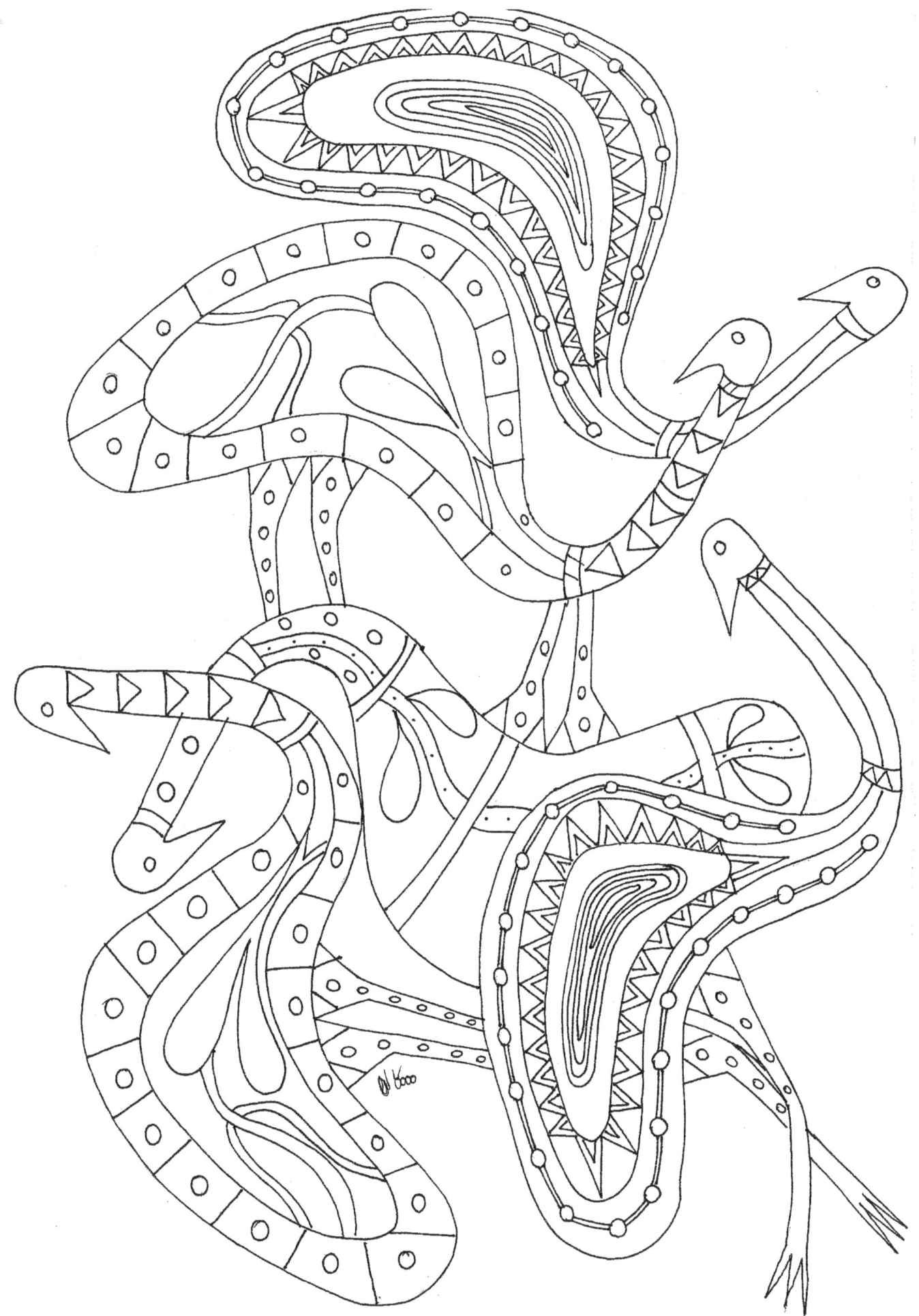

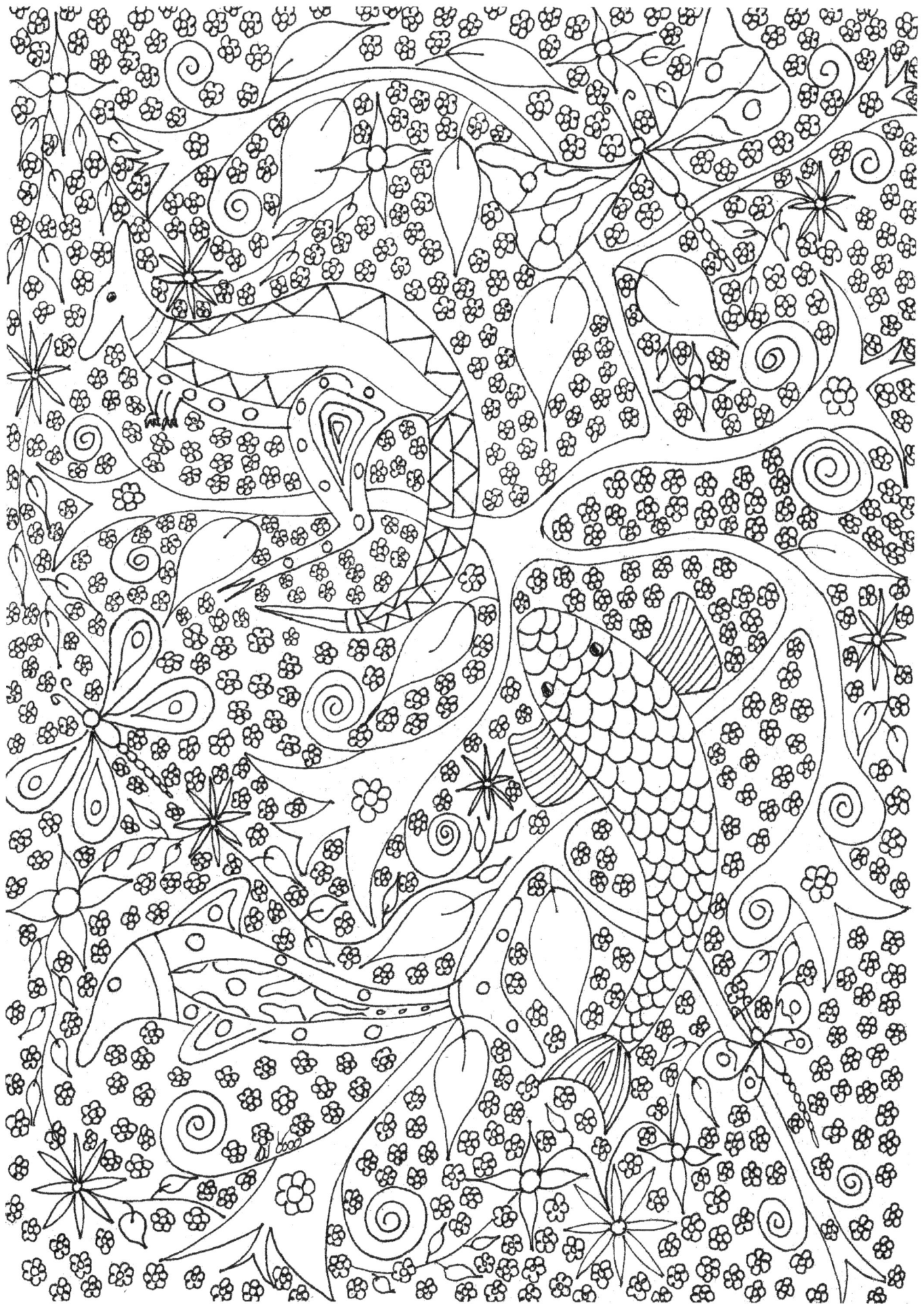

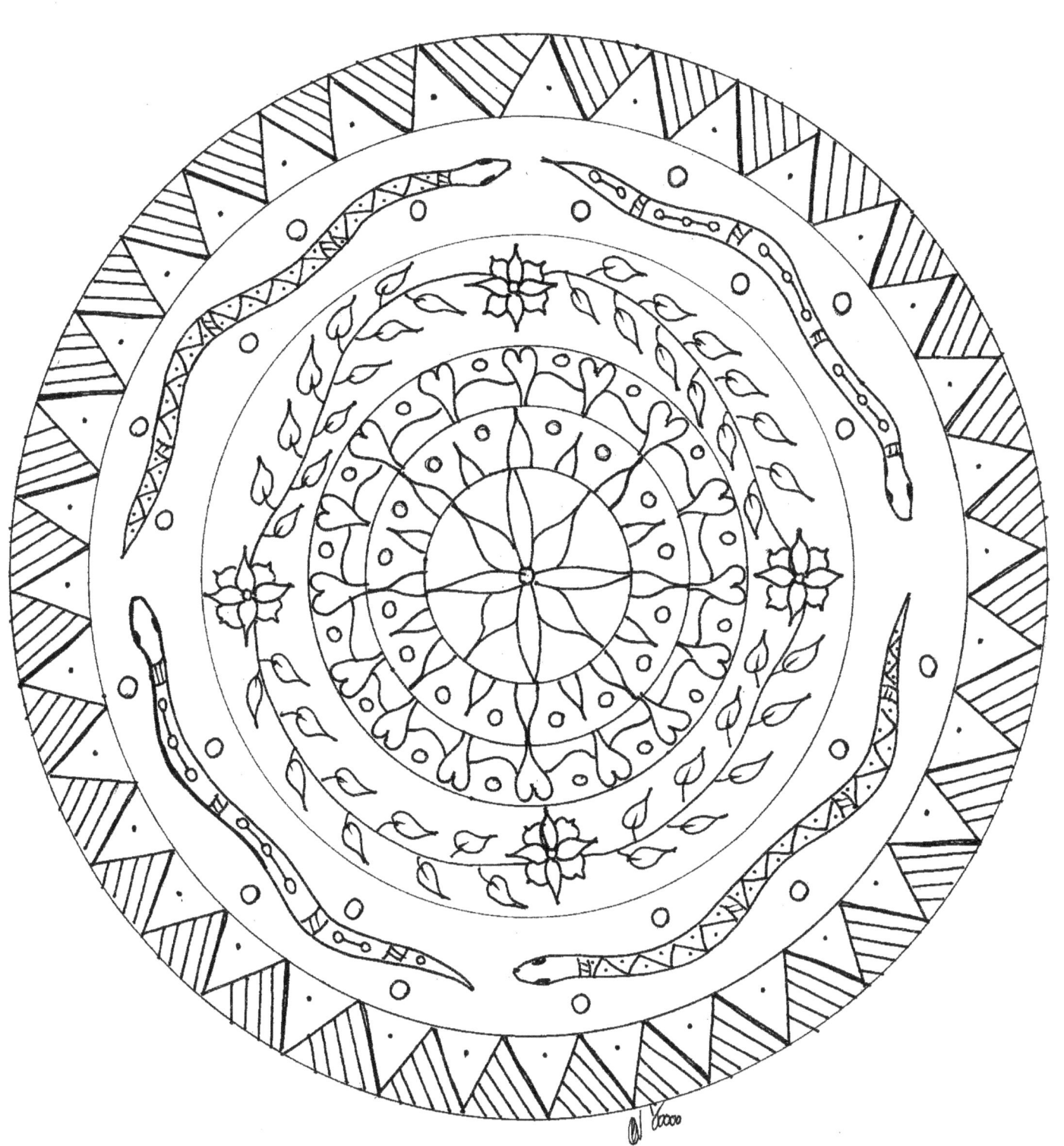

ABOUT THE AUTHOR

My name is Sharon Dawn Wortley but I prefer "Dawnie". I was born in Gunnedah NSW, daughter to Emanuel Lewis Wortley and Elizabeth Thomas (both deceased). I am the 10th child of 12 (4 deceased).

Dawnie has always been interested in Art and drawing. Initially a self-taught Artist, after completing a Diploma of Fine Arts through the Technical and Further Education college in Gunnedah, Dawnie's first major commission was a work for the first NAIDOC Debutant Ball. She has taught art to the local women's groups and at local schools and for NAIDOC events in Gunnedah. She has taught and inspired others, including a niece and nephew, who follow in her footsteps.

She became a carer for two of her nephews. Dawnie is a wonderful, giving woman, who has given her family (and community) the best of her life. She has always been there supporting her family in their pursuits often letting her own life take a back seat. Dawnie is respected by all who meet her.